W9-ARG-854

VISUAL TECHNIQUES FOR DEVELOPING SOCIAL SKILLS

TOURO COLLEGE LIBRARY
King's Hwy
WITHDRAWN

Activities and Lesson Plans for Teaching
Children with High-Functioning Autism
and Asperger's Syndrome

Rebecca Moyes, MEd

KH

Visual Techniques for Developing Social Skills
Activities and Lesson Plans for Teaching Children with High-Functioning Autism and Asperger's Syndrome

All marketing and publishing rights guaranteed to and reserved by:

FUTURE HORIZONS INC.
721 W. Abram Street
Arlington, Texas 76013
(800) 489-0727
(817) 277-0727
(817) 277-2270 (fax)
E-mail: *info@fhautism.com*
www.fhautism.com

©2011 Rebecca Moyes
Cover and interior design by Cindy Williams
All rights reserved.
Printed in the United States of America.

No part of this product may be reproduced in any manner whatsoever without written permission of Future Horizons, Inc, except in the case of brief quotations embodied in reviews.

ISBN: 9781935274513

10/28/13

Dedication

To every kid on the spectrum who struggles each day,
trying to figure out his or her social world.
I hope this book makes your life a little bit easier.

Advance Praise
for *Visual Techniques:*

This book fills an important gap in social skills instruction. It goes beyond simple explanations of skill steps and shows students in visually creative, fun ways the "why" and "how" of learning skills. I will absolutely make this book a part of my social skills programs!

Jed Baker, PhD
Director of the Social Skills Training Project
Author of *No More Meltdowns*, *Social Skills Training*, *Social Skills Picture Book*, and many more

These engaging and clear activities are fun and educational, an ideal way to teach social skills.

Dr Tony Attwood
Author of *Asperger's Syndrome* and *Exploring Feelings*

Acknowledgments

Special thanks to Chris Chemelli for her willingness to explore the idea of a social-skills group for her son...and to Billy, one terrific young man!

To all my kindred spirits at Pressley Ridge! It's a great place to work and a wonderful organization for kids.

To my family—you are the best support system a girl could ever have!

Thanks to everyone at Future Horizons—Wayne Gilpin, Jennifer Gilpin Yacio, Cindy Williams, and Heather Babiar.

And, last but not least, thanks to Jed Baker and Tony Attwood for taking the time to review and endorse this book.

Table of Contents

UNIT 3: Working Successfully with Others

Why This Book?

Important Information to Consider

I am quite convinced that there is a "right" way to teach social skills to children on the autism spectrum, and there is a "wrong" way.

First, it is important to understand that these children have a *social deficit.* Otherwise, they would not have a diagnosis of an autism spectrum disorder. In some cases, it may be that even those close to the child may not fully appreciate or understand how this social deficit will affect his or her life. Nevertheless, to receive a diagnosis of a pervasive developmental delay (PDD) disorder, a child must have symptoms that indicate social difficulty.

Recently, I had the opportunity to work with a young child by the name of Josh, who received a diagnosis of Asperger's syndrome. Although he was quite engaging, this child needed to learn the reciprocity of language. Josh had amassed a huge store of information about many topics. His method of interaction was basically talking "at" others instead of "with" others. Rarely could another child (or an adult, for that matter!) get a word in edgewise. Adults who did not know this child personally found him to be intelligent and engaging. In fact, he was so fluent with language that he passed his speech and language evaluations with flying colors. But, clearly, after several minutes of listening to his one-sided banter, it was fairly easy to see that something was different about him. Unfortunately, without some sort of intervention, his chances of developing meaningful relationships with his peers will be compromised.

Second, for most children on the spectrum, they will need to learn social skills in the same way we learn our math facts. This means they will need to practice these skills repeatedly to become proficient at using them. Unfortunately, as many of our youngsters do, sitting in front of a TV screen watching videos or playing computer games is not the way to gain these skills. In addition, since many folks with PDD do not generalize new skills well, they need to be exposed to layers of social instruction. Personally, I recommend one-on-one instruction with an adult who understands the PDD social deficit well and is willing to use visuals and other learning modalities to teach these skills. I also recommend that children with PDD have a chance to practice newly found skills with peers in small, controlled groups with structured lesson plans that allow for frequent praise and reinforcement of practiced skills.

Third, I recommend that individuals who are influential to the student in other areas of his or her life (such as the child's parents or community leaders in activities such as Boy Scouts or Girl Scouts, dance, church, or sports) learn ways to foster social interactions and reinforce appropriate attempts. Children on the spectrum may want to avoid such activities because they seem stressful or because of the sensory challenges involved. But, you can't learn to be social in a vacuum. Exposing a child to these activities in brief increments and then gradually building up to full-length sessions can help improve the child's confidence.

Fourth, I believe it is absolutely vital that schools

provide social-skills instruction, as well. Kids are in the school environment for more than 6 hours a day. Regular- and special-education teachers have so many opportunities to impart social knowledge through planned activities and incidental teaching. The school environment can provide a wealth of role models for children with PDD. The more we can reinforce the use of new skills, the more competent children will become in their use.

Last, we must remember that children with PDD disorders also have language impairment. Therefore, a "talking" type of teaching strategy is not going to be as effective as a "showing" teaching method. Children with PDD do not process language as efficiently as their non-disabled peers. That's the reason why ready-made social-skills curriculums that are heavily based on a teacher or leader reading or saying the instructions are simply not going to be as effective as lesson plans designed with visual components.

In summary, the reason for this book is threefold:

1. Social-skills instruction needs to be explicitly taught to kids with autism spectrum disorders.

2. Acquired social skills need to be rehearsed in multiple venues, hopefully using the same instructional components so that kids have a chance to generalize their skills.

3. Social-skills instruction for kids on the spectrum should include more visuals or "show-teaching" techniques, rather than language-based activities.

In your future interactions with a child on the spectrum, please make sure you consider whether he is exhibiting problematic social behavior because he is *incompetent* or because he is *noncompliant.* Consequences that are delivered because of poor social behavior without consideration that the child may be exhibiting *social incompetence because of his disability* are not appropriate. Each time a child exhibits problematic social behavior, he should be provided with additional, direct instruction so he can begin to replace these behaviors with appropriate skills. Punishment does not provide a repertoire of replacement skills; and yet, continually, this is the way children with autism are handled in school and at home when they exhibit inappropriate social skills. Just like mastering any other skills, there is a learning curve. Most kids on the spectrum will need multiple instructional opportunities and require numerous attempts to practice their skills.

There is one other piece of information that I think is important to understand: We cannot "fix" brains. Many children lack behavioral inhibition. Lots of children have executive-function deficits, along with their autism. Thus, their ability to hold instructions in short- and long-term memory, process directions, and maintain attention to task are all going to influence how successful they are at mastering the social-skills instruction that we impart. We must not forget that children's social deficits do not occur *in isolation of* their cognitive and language deficiencies. Their "total brain package" will need to be considered when designing appropriate programs. This will make it necessary for us to adapt and modify the lessons in this book so they are appropriate for all kids with PDD.

Instructions for Use:
Organizing Social Groups

Because visual instruction is so important to kids with autism spectrum disorders, each unit of this book contains lesson plans with photographs or pictures of visual supports (objects) necessary to do the lessons with the children. It is vital that you include these objects when teaching the lessons, as they help compensate for a child's language impairment.

The lesson plans can be adapted for children who are receiving the instruction as individuals or in groups. Social-skills goals to be used in the child's Individualized Education Program (IEP) are also included at the outset of each lesson. This program does not subscribe to any one particular therapy for children with autism, but there are strong components of applied behavior analysis throughout the book. *Any behavior that is reinforced is likely to continue.* Therefore, it is vital that staff identify a particular reinforcer that is effective for each child or for all the children in a group. Choosing a reinforcer that is preferred by the staff is not necessarily going to be reinforcing for the students. Incorporating students' special interests into the lesson plans is also extremely beneficial. As an example, a dragon social-skills card game ("The Dragons of Ryuu," available at *ryuuworld. com*) has been found to be very successful for kids who enjoy dragons, *Harry Potter,* or fantasy games. A child who is interested in insects might have his social-skills program adapted so he can earn books about insects or insect stickers. A useful book that discusses the power of special interests for kids on the autism spectrum is *Power Cards: Using Special Interests to Motivate Children and Youth with Asperger's Syndrome and Autism*, by Elisa Gagnon. It is a personal favorite of mine.

Many educators wonder how to set up a social-skills group that won't take away from the instructional time of the classroom. Often, these group lessons can take place during the lunch period in primary, elementary, and secondary settings. The kids simply take their lunches to eat in a different area, where there is some time to socialize and do a lesson. Try not to include just children with autism or Asperger's syndrome in the group. Kids with a social disability will need to have models of typically developing kids to make the most gains. Children with other types of social deficits (social anxiety disorder, extreme shyness, etc) can also benefit from the lessons in this book. The group can meet at other times, as well, such as before homeroom or during speech therapy sessions, club period, or study hall.

Permission will need to be obtained from the parents to enable all children to participate. You can send a letter home with your chosen students, complimenting the parents on their child's social skills and requesting permission to use them as models in a group setting that meets during lunch. Generally, such a letter will be met with much enthusiasm and pride. These are probably students that you will be able to call on for future volunteer assignments, as well. They might be willing to sit with an autistic child at a social event, engage him on the playground or during unstructured school time, or even assist him with academic tasks, such as organization or homework. Just make sure your parent permission letter gives examples of things your child might be doing to assist another child, so there are no objections later.

These students, when used to foster a host of social interactions, can become a "circle of friends" support system for the student with autism or Asperger's syndrome.

Some educators offer a volunteer certificate of participation to kids who participate in such programs in secondary settings. Many schools today require that kids obtain a certain number of volunteer hours before their graduation date. These certificates can be copied and attached to college applications. Such "clubs" are often referred to as "student buddies," "circle of friends," or "student ambassadors." As an added benefit, research shows that bullying and teasing are greatly reduced when we surround a student with social supports.

One question that continually arises is, "How much am I able to tell the typically developing kids about the students with autism in the group?" Without parental permission, you cannot discuss anything regarding a child's diagnosis. When typically developing children ask questions about the behaviors of a disabled child, care has to be taken to not divulge the child's "label." On occasion, you will find a willing parent who is able to attend the first session of the group (minus the student with autism) to help explain the disability. Some parents like to provide information in the presence of their child on the spectrum. When an educator is faced with arguments from parents who do not want other children to know their child's diagnosis, their parental wishes must always be respected. But, in my professional experience, many of the other children who interact with these kids on a regular basis already know there is something unique about the student. I can also add this note as a parent, as well: Other students are often more tolerant and supportive of a student with autism when they understand the child's deficits.

Another frequently asked question centers around who is the most qualified individual to lead the group interactions. If I had my preference, it would be a speech-language therapist with specialized training in autism and Asperger's syndrome. But, I have seen occupational therapists, guidance counselors, special-education teachers, regular-education teachers, principals, and even student teachers or education majors from local colleges run these groups successfully. For the best results, however, I think it needs to be someone who understands the symptoms of autism and Asperger's syndrome. Otherwise, when the student with Asperger's syndrome is rude or blunt, a punitive rather than instructional tone may begin to permeate. With a kid on the spectrum, we have to assume he is lacking social knowledge until we teach the replacement behaviors he needs to learn to be socially appropriate.

When the IEP team recognizes the need for forming a social-skills group, this should be written into the IEP as a *related service. Related services* are services for the child that are assigned a frequency and a location. This ensures that everyone understands this service is going to be provided to the child on a regular and predictable basis. Occasionally, a school district will want to write this as a specially designed instruction item in the IEP or as an accommodation or adaptation. Group social-skills instruction is a *service provided by an adult.* It is not an accommodation. For children with 504 plans, a social-skills group can also be included. The law does provide for the inclusion of related services in 504 plans when the 504 team recognizes a need for them in the school setting.

Unit 1
Interpersonal Interactions

Lesson 1A

Using Circle Stickers to Teach Eye Contact and Attending

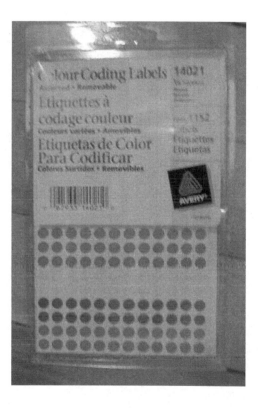

IEP Goal: "When given instruction with circle stickers, the student will be able to orient his eyes toward a speaker at a 25% higher rate than baseline data taken over the course of 3 weeks."

General Information

It is a common complaint that kids with autism do not look at people when they are speaking. We have to be sensitive to what folks on the autism spectrum say about this deficit. Many will explain that since they have language impairment, they should not be forced to look at you, or they may miss important instructions you are trying to provide through body language. In addition, many teachers and parents report that their children do not appear to be paying attention. When the children are asked a question, however, they can provide the correct answer!

In social venues, it is important that kids look at you when you speak. They may not be able to look in your eyes, but orienting to the space between your eyebrows is a great place of reference. They must be able to glean needed social information from your facial expressions, your body language, and the tone of your voice. This information gives them the knowledge they need to be able to behave appropriately. Thus, eye orientation is critical!

This activity works great as a first-day group activity, but it can also be used in the classroom on the first day of school as a means to visually teach orienting toward the teacher.

Supplies Needed

Circle stickers (You can purchase these at office supply stores.)

One large ball of yarn

Paper (one piece per student)

Pencil or pen (one for each student)

Colored cards (You can use squares of construction paper. Students should receive two cards of different colors: yellow, blue, green, or red.)

Lesson

1.   Distribute a circle sticker to each member of the group and to each adult. Everyone should place the sticker between his or her eyebrows.

2.   Every member of the group should introduce themselves, including the instructors.

3.   When all have introduced themselves, play a little game to encourage the participants to remember names. Stand behind a child, point to his head, and encourage the kids to shout out the child's name. Do this repeatedly and randomly, until all children appear to know the names of those participating.

4.   Say, "Boys and girls, you are probably wondering why we are all wearing these stickers between our eyebrows. The stickers are reminders. When we are speaking with someone, we should look toward the sticker. It makes the speaker feel special and

important. Everyone likes to feel special and important."

5. At this point, it is useful to begin delivering reinforcers to kids that are doing a great job at looking and continuing to look. The reinforcers could be either a token that adds up to "earning" a preferred reinforcer (called a "token economy" system) or the actual reinforcer itself.

6. Say, "Now we are going to play a game. This game requires that you really pay attention to what someone is trying to say through their eyes and through their actions, because you will not be allowed to speak while we are playing this game!"

7. "Right now, I want you to pretend that you can't talk. The only way that you can communicate is through your hands and your body. I want you to put yourselves in one big line according to the month you were born. So, if you were born in January, you will be at the front of the line. If you were born in December, you will be at the back of the line. If two of you are born in the same month, then the person who was born earliest in that month should go ahead of the other in line. Do you understand? When the group is all in line, and you are all satisfied that the line is in correct order, you should all put your thumbs up like this (demonstrate "thumbs up").

8. Answer any questions briefly so that all are clear on the directions. Have the kids stand up for the activity. Stress the importance of eye contact. Then say, "Ready? Go!"

9.   Give the kids several minutes to try to organize themselves in line. When all thumbs are up, see if they arranged themselves correctly.

10.   Say, "Do you think you could have done that activity without looking at the people in your group?" (Discuss why or why not.)

11.   Reiterate, "As we said earlier, when you look at someone, you make them feel important."

12.   "Now, we are going to play another activity that will help us learn about the members of this group. Remember, we need to help each other feel important, so be sure to look at the stickers of those around you!"

13.   Distribute two differently colored cards to each student in the group.

14.   Say, "Now, I am going to ask everyone who has a certain color to stand. I am then going to ask a question for those who are standing. The rest of you should pay attention to their answers, because there will be a quiz at the end of the class—and whoever has the most correct answers wins the game!"

15.   "If you have a yellow card, please stand." (Kids will stand.)

16.   Ask, "What is your favorite food?" Each kid standing will state his favorite food. Reinforce good eye contact. Have one adult write the names of the kids down, along with their favorite foods, under a "Favorite Food" column on a piece of paper. This

information will be used for the quiz later.

17. Say, "OK, you can sit down. Now, everyone who has a green card, please stand." (Kids will stand.)

18. "What is your favorite thing to do after school?" Each kid standing will state his favorite activity. Continue to reinforce good eye contact. An adult should continue to write down answers under a second column that says "Favorite Activity."

19. Say, "OK, you can sit down. Now, everyone who has a red card, please stand." (Kids will stand.)

20. Ask, "What do you want to be when you grow up?" You can also use the words "career choice" for older kids. Each kid standing will state what he wants to be. Continue to reinforce good eye contact. An adult should write down the responses under a third column that says "Career Choice."

21. Say, "OK, you can sit down. Finally, anyone who has a blue card, please stand." (Kids will stand.)

22. Ask, "What kind of pets do you have? If you don't have any, just say, 'I don't have any.'" Each kid standing will list their pets. Again, continue to reinforce good eye contact, and have an adult write down the responses under a fourth column that says "Pets."

23. Distribute a piece of paper and a pencil or pen to each student. Say, "Now we are going to see who was paying attention the best! When I ask a question, write down the appropriate name of a student from our game. For example, I might say, 'Who has

a cat?' Then you should write down the name of a person who said they have a cat."

24. Using the information from the adult who took notes, briefly compose a five-point quiz to see who was listening. Reward the student who has the most points.

25. Say, "OK, now we have one more activity. Remember, we need to be looking at each other's stickers. For this activity, we will have to sit in a circle." Facilitate the kids sitting down in a circle on the floor.

26. Say, "For this game, we need a volunteer to start us off. Do I have a volunteer?" (One student will need to start the game off.)

27. "What I want you [the volunteer] to do is say one thing that you do really well. I want you to say, 'My name is _____, and I am really good at _____.' Then, I want you to roll this ball of yarn to another student, but keep holding onto a piece of the yarn as it rolls away."

28. Demonstrate this yourself, stating what you really enjoy, and then roll the yarn to your volunteer so that he or she can go next.

29. Continue the game until all have had a chance to get the yarn. To end the game, the yarn should be rolled back to the first student. Adults in the room should reinforce good eye contact.

30. Say, "Now that we have all had a turn, I want you to stand up while you hold onto your yarn. Don't let

go! Look how we have all become tangled up with each other! Let's all take a step backward, making our yarn web get tighter. See how strong our yarn web has become, because we have all stuck together? Now, let's have our volunteer drop his/her piece." (The leader drops his piece.)

31. "Do you see how the whole group was affected because one person quit the activity? That's how it is when one person doesn't try hard with the group or gives up. The whole group feels it. So, for next time, I want you to try hard to remember the names of the people in this group and to look toward other people's eyes so they feel special."

32. Distribute reinforcers for the kids who earned them. If you used a token economy system, the more tokens the student earned, the more value his reinforcer should have. As the kids move on to other classrooms or venues, be sure that their teachers and parents continue to reinforce eye contact. Otherwise, the student will learn to use eye contact only when he is with you!

Lesson 1B
Using Carpet Mats and Masking Tape to Teach Personal Space When Sitting

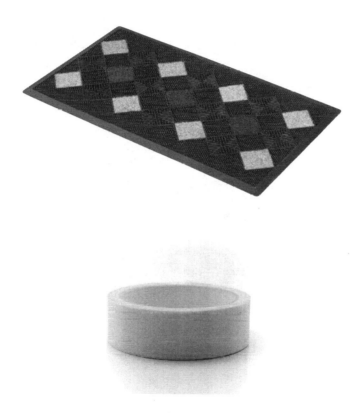

IEP Goal: "When given a carpet mat and/or a desk border defined with masking tape, the student will demonstrate an improvement from baseline data in keeping his body confined to appropriate boundaries in 7 out of 10 random daily observations."

General Information

Many times, kids with autism are reprimanded for invading others' personal space. They may stand too close when they talk to another person, walk on the back of others' heels, or have their arms and legs "all over the place" when they are required to sit in confined areas, such as "circle time." They often have difficulty recognizing where their space ends and another's begins. This can be seen at the lunch table, where they may have their lunch spread out over several seats, or when their belongings are all over the floor, blocking aisles or hallways. It may also be observed in academic settings, where student desks are pushed together "table style." The student with autism or Asperger's syndrome may lean over onto others' desks or get his belongings mixed up with those of the student next to him.

A simple solution to this problem may be outlining the student's desk with masking tape so he recognizes where his boundaries are. If the children around him do not seem to have this problem, then just outline the desk of the student who has the problem. This will help to make it more visually defined for him.

If a child has a problem demonstrating appropriate personal space while seated on the floor, you can require him to sit on a carpet mat. He should be instructed to keep his body within the confines of the mat. (For one kindergarten student with Asperger's syndrome who had this difficulty, his teacher explained that the mat was similar to Aladdin's magic carpet and that he had to keep his body on the mat.)

It's critical to remember that while the student is mastering this skill, you must reinforce his attempts to be appropriate, as well as encourage the other children to do the same. One cannot expect a child with autism to conform to appropriate social norms while the other students "get away" with demonstrating the same problem.

The next page contains a social tale that can be read to a child to explain why appropriate personal space is important. The story is intended for a student beyond second grade. Before reading the tale to the student(s), you can demonstrate what good personal space looks like when you are seated at your desk. Use an actual desk to role-play this. Then demonstrate what inappropriate social space looks like while seated at the desk. Ask other kids to demonstrate it, as well, one at a time. Then, demonstrate what appropriate and inappropriate personal space looks like when seated in a small, confined area on the floor. Perhaps you can use the phrase "criss-cross applesauce" to encourage children to cross their legs so they have a good visual of what is expected when they sit in a group on the floor. Then, you can provide the students with carpet mats to practice the skills. With the carpet mats, have students demonstrate inappropriate personal space and appropriate personal space. Then, reinforce the appropriate personal space.

Supplies Needed

One carpet mat for each child (Many carpet dealers are willing to donate old sample colors. You can also purchase inexpensive entry mats at a dollar store.)

Masking tape

A copy of the social tale (One for each student. You can also provide a copy of the tale to each student's parents for review at home.)

A Social Tale about Personal Space

Personal space is the amount of vacant (empty) air between you and another person.

Everyone needs personal space.

When we don't get enough personal space, we may feel crowded.

When I am too close to another person, it may make them feel uncomfortable because I am not giving them personal space.

If I lean over my desk onto other students' desks, it may also make them feel uncomfortable.

If I stretch out my hands and legs when I am in a small group seated on the floor, this may also make some people feel uncomfortable.

I will try to keep my hands and body within the masking-tape outline of my desk.

I will also try to keep my hands and body inside my carpet mat when seated on the floor with a group.

In this way, I will help everyone to feel comfortable.

I will feel comfortable too!

Lesson 1C
Using Hula-Hoops to Teach Personal Space

IEP Goal: "When given instruction with a Hula-Hoop, the student will be able to exhibit an improvement from baseline data in demonstrating appropriate personal space during conversations, while waiting in lines, and while moving through lines."

General Instructions

Hula-Hoops make excellent visuals that can easily demonstrate the way each person needs personal space in front of them and behind them. Some children exhibit problems with following someone too closely. They constantly walk on the back of others' shoes, and, oftentimes, the person they are following will feel crowded or like they are being "hovered" over.

Hula-Hoops have been around a long time and can be purchased fairly inexpensively in dollar stores or in the toy section of major department stores. Providing each student with one is very helpful! They are most commonly available during the spring and summer months, so you may have to plan ahead to purchase them. They can be stored easily by using a long nail to hang them on the back of a door in a storage closet.

The picture on page 27 demonstrates how kids can learn about personal space in a seated position. The boy on the left is demonstrating the use of the hoop correctly. The boy sitting forward in the middle is not using the hoop appropriately. The hoop should fit over the back of the chair. This lesson plan could then continue by teaching the concepts of personal space in a standing line and a moving line. It would also be important to discuss times when maintaining personal space is difficult. Some examples would be a crowded church pew, an elevator, or a long ticket line. Wording to this effect could be added to the social tale on page 25.

Supplies Needed

Hula-Hoops (One for each student. Try to purchase the larger type.)

Note: The following lesson should be done in a group with several students.

Seated Personal Space Lesson

1. Say, "Boys and girls, today we are going to continue to learn about personal space. Who remembers what personal space is?" (Solicit responses.)

2. "We talked before about how it is important to keep your hands and your feet within your desk borders or on the floor on your carpet mat. Now, we are going to talk about the personal space behind and in front of you."

3. "How many of you have ever accidentally walked behind someone and then, suddenly, you walked on their shoe and it came off? Was the person angry with you when this happened?" (Solicit responses.) "If this seems to happen a lot, it may be that you are walking too close."

4. "How many of you have ever ridden in the back seat of a small car?" (Solicit responses.)

5. "What happens when the person in front of you leans his seat back too far?" (Solicit responses.)

6. "I am going to have you sit back in your chair now and put a Hula-Hoop around your middle."

7. Distribute the hoops and model how they should fit over each child, making sure the Hula-Hoops slide over the back of the chairs. The kids should see that personal space extends beyond the back of the chairs.

8. "The Hula-Hoop represents how much space you should have between you and another person. Take a look behind you. Do you see how your Hula-Hoop gives you space behind you, as well?"

9. At this point, role-play inappropriate personal space while seated, using students in your group as models. The following demonstrations are good examples to do; however, feel free to role-play situations that you have seen, as well. Slip the Hula-Hoops over the students to demonstrate visually how they have violated personal space.

Inappropriate Personal Space Demonstrations

- A child who sits in a chair is being bothered by someone from behind. The second child is leaning in too close, tapping his shoulder, or using a pencil to touch his hair.

- A child sitting in the front leans back too far into the space of the child behind him.

- A child turns sideways in his chair and rests his elbow on the desk of the child behind him.

Standing Personal Space Lesson

1.   Say, "Now, sometimes we have to wait in lines. A 'waiting line' is when we have to wait to move somewhere else. An example would be waiting to buy an ice cream cone at the Dairy Queen. Another example would be waiting to purchase a ticket or waiting to get into a movie. Can you think of others?" (Solicit examples.)

2.   Line the kids up, and have each of them put their Hula-Hoops around them so there is equal space in front of and behind them.

3.   Say, "This is how you should stand in a waiting line. You do not want people in front of or behind you to be offended because they feel crowded. Naturally, you won't have your Hula-Hoops with you, so a good way to make sure you aren't too close is to hold out your hand in the front and rotate it around behind you. That will help you know just how much empty space you need to keep around you." (Have the kids do this.)

4.   At this point, it might be useful to talk about exceptions to personal space in a waiting line. For instance, in a small foyer, where there is only a small space for people to wait, someone would have to stand in the cold or the rain if people didn't pack in tighter. Another example would be an elevator. Discuss how important it would be for the student to behave appropriately in a situation like that. Then, have the kids model this type of situation so they can "see" it.

Personal Space in a Moving Line Lesson

1. Say, "Once the line starts to move, you should remember what we talked about: not walking too closely to someone. You should also not leave a large gap between you and the person in front of you as you walk. Why is this not appropriate?" (Solicit responses.) You could explain to the students that moving lines are moving somewhere. Usually people want to get there quickly. Dawdling along or taking your time might irritate people. You should emphasize that running is not OK, either!

2. Have the kids practice moving throughout the building, holding their Hula-Hoops with their hands on the right and left sides to balance the hoops so there is equal space in the front of and behind them.

Note: Be sure to keep reinforcing the practice of appropriate personal space!

Lesson 1D
Teaching Respect for Belongings and Territories as Related to Personal Space

IEP GOAL: "When given visual instruction on personal 'territories' and 'belongings,' the student will demonstrate an improvement from baseline data in exhibiting respect for others' personal space."

General Information

Some children have great difficulty with impulse control. When faced with a temptation, they will "go for it" without thinking through the consequences of their behavior. In other words, the "good angel" that says to them, "You'd better wait until you have permission!" or "If I do this, I could get in big trouble!" seems to be outweighed by the "bad angel" that says, "Go for it!" This is an example of a lack of behavioral inhibition. They appear to lack that special something that inhibits them from being inappropriate. Behavioral inhibition is an executive-function deficit. Sometimes behavioral inhibition can be taught; other times, the brain dysfunction is too severe, and mastering this social skill is too difficult. However, as educators we should always try to teach replacement skills for problematic behaviors, and this lesson plan teaches children about behavioral inhibition.

When faced with temptation, many students will succumb. As an example, a cafeteria tray that contains a student's favorite foods or drinks may be too much to refrain from touching. Getting into another student's desk, backpack, or purse can also create big social problems for a student with autism.

A book, backpack, calculator, pencil, purse, and wallet are all examples of "belongings" (possessions). "Belongings" are owned by other people. But, what people find offensive is when they see that someone has gotten into their purse, their wallet, or their backpack uninvited. So, although they are belongings, they are also "forbidden territories." A desk drawer, a mailbox, someone's bedroom, or a computer may also be belongings, but they are territories that an individual must learn to respect to avoid trouble, as well.

One teacher that I worked with in a classroom for more disabled autistic students used M&M'S and other food items as reinforcers. The M&M'S were clearly visible in a jar on her desk. Often, a few students with poor executive-functioning skills would walk up to her desk and grab a handful. Thus, the M&M'S were losing their power as a reinforcer because the kids had full access to them. She didn't want to "hide" them—she wanted the kids to learn that they were off-limits, except when she delivered them. She identified one student who had this habit. She put one M&M on his desk. She used the phrase "No Touch!" firmly and covered the M&M with her hand. The student was instructed to get out a pencil (a very quick task that he could complete easily). If the student was able to complete the task and refrain from touching the M&M, he earned verbal praise ("Nice job waiting!") and was then given two extra M&M'S, along with the one on the desk. If he grabbed the M&M and ate it before completing the task, he only got one—the one he ate without permission. If he grabbed the M&M and ate it, the teacher would show another one to the student, hold it up in her hand, cover her hand, and then say, "No Touch!". Then, she would immediately issue a verbal directive to get out his pencil. Gradually, the tasks were lengthened in duration, and the student learned that if he waited and completed his task, his reinforcer was even better than before.

Here is a good activity to help students learn about impulse control.

Supplies Needed

A variety of "belongings," as well as some examples of "territories" (You might be able to replicate the contents of a cafeteria tray by using a tray and some plastic food and utensils.)

Wipe-off board, flip chart, or blackboard to write on

Lesson

1. Say, "Boys and girls, last time, we discussed personal space. There are other types of personal space, as well. One is called 'Belongings Space.' We can also refer to belongings as *possessions*."

2. "Let's write the names of some of our belongings or possessions on the board."

3. Students can each write the names of the items they think of on the board, or they can call them out and you can write them.

4. Say, "I want you to tell me one thing that you don't like people taking from you or borrowing from you without asking." (Let all the kids say one item.)

5. Say, "Guess what? Almost EVERYONE doesn't like it when you borrow things or take things of theirs without asking. Some people even get upset when you get too close to their stuff without touching it. So, you should not handle, touch, or get into other people's belongings or possessions for any reason unless you have their permission."

6. "Let's do some role-playing so we can demonstrate what that looks like."

7. Choose several students to act out the following skits.

Note: These scenarios would be great to videotape and replay for the students. This method of instruction is referred to as "video modeling."

- Two students are sitting together, playing with a toy owned by one of the students. The owner is holding the toy, and the other student is watching. The owner leaves for a moment, comes back, and finds the other student playing with his toy. Brainstorm with the student who owns the toy and the one who doesn't. Discuss how the second student violated "belongings space."

- Two students are using their calculators. One student reaches over and grabs the other student's calculator. Discuss how the second student violated "belongings space."

- Two students are doing homework. One student takes the other person's homework and starts to copy it. Discuss how the second student violated "belongings space."

(Note: The correct way to do the above could also be videotaped.)

8. Say, "Now, sometimes belongings are important to people because there is privacy connected to them. For instance, your mom's wallet is a belonging—it belongs to her, but getting into it and seeing how much money your mom has is also a violation of her privacy. A wallet is *your mom's territory*. And you don't belong in someone else's territory, unless you have his or her permission."

9.   "Let's write some examples of 'territories' on the board." You might write:

Your tray in the cafeteria

Your backpack

Your desk

Your coat pockets

Your purse

10. Remind the kids that when something is out of sight, it's a good idea to keep it that way. It's usually not meant to be shared with everyone.

11. Say, "Now, let's role-play some of these territory space violations." (Choose some students to role-play the following scenarios. Again, videotaping the scenarios would make them even more visual.)

   • Two kids are eating lunch. One kid reaches over and takes something off the other kid's tray.

   • One kid gets into another kid's backpack for a piece of candy.

   • One kid opens his teacher's purse to look around.

   • One kid needs crayons. He begins to search in everyone's desk for some.

12. Say, "So, in summary, it's important to remember that we do not touch other people's belongings without asking first, and we don't get into other people's territories without asking first!"

41

Unit 2
Appropriate Communication

Lesson 2A
Using a Colander to Teach
Filtering of Thoughts to Avoid
Inappropriate Language

IEP Goal: "When given instruction with a colander, the student will demonstrate a 50% improvement in screening out the use of offensive words around peers, according to baseline data acquired in 10 observations during nonstructured times of the day over a 3-week period."

General Information

As was mentioned earlier, a lack of behavioral inhibition arises from executive-function deficits. Children with autism spectrum disorders are known to have this problem, but so do others with cognitive impairment. We often observe this among our elderly folks: They too lose the ability to "filter." Individuals with executive-function impairment are often blunt and rude in their interactions. Sometimes, when they are corrected for such behavior, they appear shocked and hurt. After all, they feel that they were just conveying some tidbit of truthful information!

Kids on the spectrum must learn to filter their thoughts and make judgments about how another person will receive their remarks. Often, the problem is twofold: First, the child has difficulty screening his thoughts to avoid inappropriate comments, and, second, the child has difficulty predicting what may happen as a result of uttering those inappropriate comments. We will address the second part of this dilemma in a later chapter.

This lesson also relates to the popular idiom of "putting your foot in your mouth." A visual of a large foot could also be used if the meaning of this idiom were to be discussed. With this lesson, it is also helpful if the instructor knows beforehand what sort of unkind words the child with autism frequently says (eg, he frequently calls people "stupid") so that these words can be added to a list of words that students are not allowed to use in the classroom. This may seem offensive, but we are striving for concrete, direct instruction.

"Unkind" words fall into several categories, and these can be useful to teach, as well. Some categories to consider would be *insult words.* You can discuss the various subcategories of insults, such as comments related to weight, religion, skin color, intelligence, and race. *Curse words* would be another category. Many children use *self-deprecating words*; such language is unkind to the "self." This category can be added, as well. *Bragging words* can also be unkind. Finally, a category having to do with *privacy violation words* can be added. When a student makes remarks or asks questions that violate someone else's privacy (eg, "How much do you weigh?" or "How much money do you make?" or "Are you pregnant?"), this too can be unkind talk.

You can also make a "kind words" category. There are plenty of things to write here, as well! *Warm and friendly greetings* are kind words. *Helpful words* (eg, "That looks heavy—let me carry that for you!") and *caring words* (eg, "You were sick for two days! Are you feeling better?") can also be added as subcategories to the "kind words" category. *Compliments* could be another subcategory.

Another practical way to teach "kind words" and "unkind words" is to use colors. "Kind words" could be "green words" (ie, "Go!"), and "unkind words" could be "red words" (ie, "Stop!"). A group activity could include role-playing what you should do when you discover that your filtering ability has failed, and you have hurt someone's feelings. Videotaping a skit where someone has done this and now must rectify the damage is a perfect way to "show-teach" this skill.

Supplies Needed

Colander or strainer

Three cups of sand, mixed with some medium-sized pebbles

Cup or dipper to scoop the sand and pebbles up in

Container to catch the sand once it filters through the colander

Piece of paper with a large green square on it

Piece of paper with a large red square on it, a flip chart, and markers (You may also use a blackboard or wipe-off board. If using a flip chart or wipe-off board, you may also want to use a green marker and a red marker.)

For group activities, use some note cards with scenarios of unkind and kind word situations written out.

Lesson

1. Say, "Have you ever said something that got you into trouble? Here's an example: Someone asks you if they look nice. You don't think they do, so you tell them so. Then they are hurt by what you said, and you got into trouble for saying it. You thought you were being honest, but the other person's feelings were hurt. Has anyone ever had that happen?" (Solicit responses.)

2. Hold up the colander. Say, "What is this thing? What

is it used for?" (Discuss how spaghetti is made to demonstrate that the noodles stay in, and the hot water gets filtered out.)

3. Say, "I am going to give a demonstration, and I want you to pay close attention." Pour some sand and pebbles through the colander. Say, "Do you see how the sand filters through the colander, and the pebbles are left behind?"

4. "The colander is a lot like our brains. When we are thinking about things to say, our brain helps us decide if what we are going to say is appropriate or not. We shouldn't always say the first thing that our brain THINKS. We need to *filter* our thoughts. The sand is like our *kind words*—we can let *kind words come out*. But the rocks are like our *mean words*— we need to keep them in our brains and *not let them out*. They are hard, and they hurt people."

5. Let the kids take turns doing the colander and sand activity, then have them take a seat near the flip chart, blackboard, or wipe-off board.

6. On the board, write two headings for two columns: "Kind Words" and "Unkind Words." Beside "Kind Words," draw a flower and a candy bar. Beside "Unkind Words," draw a garbage can. Explain that *kind words* make people feel good—just like if someone gives you flowers or candy. You feel happy to receive these things! *Unkind words* are trash words. They are dirty, and they make people feel gross, just like the stuff in a garbage can.

7. Say, "Now we are going to give you some guidelines on what *kind words* are and what *unkind words* are. Let's start with *kind words*."

8.   *"Kind words* make people feel good. One type of *kind word* is called a c*ompliment. Compliments* are words that we say to another person to make them feel special. There are different types of compliments, and we will talk about this later. An example of a compliment might be, 'Hey, you did a great job on that test!' or 'I really like your new shirt!'"

9.   Write "Compliments" under the "Kind Words" heading on the board. Solicit examples of compliments from the kids, and write a few off to the side.

10.   Say, "Another example of kind words is *helping words.* When you offer to help someone with something, such as holding the door, showing them how to do something, or picking up something they dropped on the floor, these are all ways to make someone feel good. You can say, 'Do you need help?' or, if you can see that they do, you can say, 'Let me help you!'"

11.   Write "Helping Words" on the board. Solicit some examples from the kids and write them off to the side.

12.   Say, "Another type of kind word is a *green word.*" Write "Green Words" with a green marker under the "Kind Words" heading on the board.

13.   Hold up the paper with the green square, and say, "*Green words* are words that are said with warmth and happiness. It's not so much the words that you choose, but the way you say them." Model a warm and friendly greeting, versus an unfriendly greeting, by changing the tone of your voice. Say, "Do you hear how my voice makes it *sound* friendly?"

14. Say, "Here are some other *green words*: 'Welcome back!' or 'Yeah! You're here!' or 'How are you?' or 'Sit here!'"

15. Have the kids contribute other *green word* ideas and write them on the board.

16. Say, "The important thing to remember is that when you use *kind words*, they will make YOU feel good too, because, usually, when you use them, people will remember that YOU are a nice person and will treat you nicely too!"

17. "Now, let's work on the 'Unkind Words' side. *Unkind words* make people feel bad. One type of *unkind word* is called an *insult*. An *insult* is when you say something to someone that makes them feel bad about the type of person they are. An example would be to call someone 'stupid.' This word makes them feel that they aren't smart. Another example would be to call someone 'ugly.' This word may make them feel unattractive. Can you think of some other *insults*?"

18. Write "Insults" under the "Unkind Words" heading on the board. Off to the side, you can write some insulting words that students share.

19. Say, "The next type of 'Unkind Words' is called *threats*. *Threats* are when we tell people that we are going to do or might do something that will hurt them or someone they love. An example would be, 'I'm going to shoot you' or 'I'm going to kill you.' *Threats* make people afraid, and being afraid to come to school or to go home is not a good feeling, is it?"

20. Write "Threats" under the "Unkind Words" heading on the board. Solicit some additional threats from the students and write them off to the side.

21. Say, "Finally, I am going to write 'Red Words' under this heading, as well. Mean comments are 'Red Words.'" Hold up the paper with the red square. Say, "Mean comments are words that we say in anger or when we are frustrated. They also cause people to feel alone. An example of a mean comment, or a *red word,* is 'I hate you' or 'You aren't my friend anymore' or 'Get out of here.' Mean comments can make people feel that they are by themselves, and no one likes that feeling."

22. Write "Red Words" with a red marker under the "Unkind Words" heading on the board. Solicit some additional examples from kids and write them off to the side.

23. Say, "Now, occasionally, we will all say an *unkind word.* We do this because sometimes, it just slips out. Our colander didn't work. This happens to everyone. What should you do when you say an *unkind word*?" (Solicit responses.)

24. "Whenever you realize that you said an *unkind word*, you should immediately say you are sorry. You should say, 'I didn't mean to say that, and I'm sorry.' But, what if you didn't realize it was an *unkind word*? How will you know that it was?" (Solicit responses.)

25. "You will realize it was an *unkind word* if the person begins to cry, starts yelling at you, or tells the teacher on you. At that point, you can also say, 'I'm sorry.'"

26. At this point, you can do some role-playing with note cards that have scenarios of *unkind* and *kind* words written on them. These scenarios would be great to videotape, as well. Suggestions might be:

- Some kids are playing a board game together. One kid wins, and the other loses. The winner says, "I won! Ha, ha!!!!" and starts dancing around. This is an example of using *red words*. These comments make the loser feel alone.

- A kid is carrying a stack of books, and another kid offers to help. This is an example of using *helping words*.

- It's report card day, and several kids are looking at their report cards. One kid starts to cry. Another kid says, "Don't worry—you will do better next time!" This is an example of using *helping words*.

- Two kids arrive at school in the morning. One kid says, "Hey, I like your shirt!" to the other. This is an example of a *compliment*.

- One kid is new to the school. Another kid says, "I heard you were new to our school. Do you want to eat with me today at lunch?" This is an example of using *green words*.

Lesson 2B
Using a Pitcher to Teach Compliments as Kind Words

IEP Goal: "When given instruction in the four types of compliments, the student will be able to deliver a compliment to a peer in group sessions in four out of five opportunities."

General Information

This lesson is a great addition to Lesson 2A and is designed particularly for students who have difficulty using kind and friendly language with peers. Delivering a compliment can also be an effective way to initiate a conversation with others. It can be a precursor to building a friendship. Complimenting others has a twofold effect: The receiver of compliments benefits, and the giver does, too. This lesson plan is derived from the book, *How Full Is Your Bucket,* by Tom Rath and Mary Reckmeyer (Gallup Press; 2009). The story is for elementary-aged children but can be adapted for teens, as well.

Children with autism need to become adept at understanding why compliments should be used and what type of compliments there are. Direct instruction in compliments can be delivered to the student individually or in a group session.

Since a compliment is often delivered spontaneously, it is hard to capture with data collection. For this reason, noting student improvement in the use of compliments may be hard to measure. However, there are several ways to track improvement.

First, during group practice, the instructor could record the number of successes in delivering the compliment to a peer on demand. But, this method will not capture whether the student is able to do this spontaneously.

If a social skills group has been created, typically developing students in the group may be asked to note if particular children have delivered a compliment to them outside of the group session. You can speak with the student on the spectrum about the expectation that he should strive to compliment several kids. Provide him with the names of a few classmates. By asking these students if compliments were delivered, we can attempt to discover if he or she is demonstrating this skill in generalized settings. Or, teachers can be alerted to the type of data collection that is being sought and asked to be observant about whether the student has demonstrated this skill. Further, students themselves can be provided with a recording sheet to write down who they have complimented, the date, and what type of compliment they used. I've provided an example in Table 2.1.

Children with autism spectrum disorders often need to "buy into" the idea of why the use of appropriate social skills is necessary. So, it will be helpful if success in the use of compliments earns a meaningful reinforcer for the student.

Supplies Needed

Flip chart

Markers

Note cards

Bucket (any color) filled with water

A clear, empty pitcher

Dipper or ladle

Recording chart

Lesson

1. Say, "Today, we are going to continue our discussion about kind words and unkind words. How many of you have had some unkind words said to you recently?" (Solicit responses.) "How did they make you feel?"

2. "I am going to demonstrate something to you now. Do you see this empty pitcher?" (Hold it up.) "Let's assume this pitcher represents how you are feeling when you start your day."

3. "Every time someone says something nice to you, good feelings are added to your pitcher. You start to feel happy and proud. Let's assume that the water I am adding to the pitcher represents our happy thoughts."

4. Use the dipper to move several helpings of water from the bucket to the pitcher.

5. "Now, let's say someone says or does something mean to you. With each mean thing that is said to you, your pitcher becomes depleted. You start to feel unhappy. And when people ignore you, or when they don't say anything at all to you, it can work the same way."

6. Use the dipper to move some water from the pitcher back to the bucket.

7. Put the pitcher, bucket, and dipper aside.

8. "Now, I am going to show you about a way to help keep other people's pitchers full. It has to do with using kind words, and these kind words are called

compliments."

9.   Write "PAPA" vertically on the flip chart, with each letter going down the left side of the chart.

10. Say, "The letter 'P' stands for *possessions.*" Write "Possessions" on the flip chart beside the "P." Say, "*Possessions* are belongings. We can compliment someone on something that belongs to them. An example would be, 'I like your new video game!' or 'I like your purse.'"

11. "Can you turn to the person next to you and give them a *possession compliment* to help fill up their pitcher?"

12. Say, "'A' stands for *appearance.*" Write "Appearance" on the flip chart beside the "A." Say, "This type of compliment helps to fill up someone's pitcher, because you are complimenting the way they look. Complimenting what someone is wearing can also be an *appearance compliment.* An example would be, 'I love your new haircut!' or 'You look so nice today!'"

13. "Can you turn to the person next to you and give them an *appearance compliment* to help fill up their pitcher?"

14. "'P' stands for *personality.*" Write "Personality" on the flip chart beside the next "P." Say, "A person's personality is the way they act or who they are. They might be friendly, smart, a hard worker, a good studier, athletic, or a great dancer. So, when you compliment someone's personality, you could say, 'You are such a hard worker!' or 'You are so smart!' or 'I wish I could be as musical as you are!' To be

able to compliment someone with a *personality compliment*, you have to know them, or you have to observe something that they do well. This is the hardest compliment to use, but it really fills up people's pitchers if you can use it. Does anyone have an idea of a *personality compliment* for someone in this group?" (Solicit responses.)

15. "'A' stands for *achievement*." Write "Achievement" on the flip chart beside the last "A." Say, "This is an easy compliment to give someone. Whenever someone does something very well, you can give them a compliment about it. Here are some examples: 'You did a great job on that test!' or 'Wow, you played that game so well!' or 'Congratulations on the track meet!' Does anyone have an idea of an *achievement compliment* to share with the group?" (Solicit responses.)

16. "Now, if you look at the flip chart, we have spelled the word 'PAPA.' Using PAPAs helps to fill other people's pitchers, as well as your own. Why does it fill your pitcher too?" (Solicit responses. What you are trying to achieve is the realization that when you make others feel good, this in turn helps them to realize you are a nice person. This will result in more positive social interactions."

17. At this point, you can have the kids select from a stack of 3 x 5 cards. Some cards should have a compliment written on them, and the students can take turns saying what type of compliment it is by using the chart on the board. Other cards should have a directive that they have to deliver a certain type of compliment to a peer in their group or to state a compliment. Each student should take turns

reading his or her card out loud to the group and then perform the requested task.

18. At the conclusion of the session, provide each student with a recording chart. The chart should consist of the date, the compliment they said, and the name of the person they delivered the compliment to. The students should strive to deliver five compliments before the next session and turn the chart in at the start of the next class.

Table 2.1.
Sample Recording Chart for Delivering Compliments

DATE	PERSON	WRITE THE COMPLIMENT SAID

Lesson 2C
Using a Speedometer to Teach Appropriate Volume and Speed When Speaking

IEP Goal: "When provided with a visual prompt (a scale or speedometer), the student will be able to self-regulate his voice to the appropriate speed and volume during four out of five problematic times."

General Information

The music of the voice is termed *prosody*. For one reason or another, the prosody of a student's voice may be cause for concern.

Some children with autism exhibit voices that sound high or "squeaky." Others use a voice that sounds much lower or older than their years. Some children speak too quickly, and others too slowly. There are kids who whisper when they speak, and those who talk too loudly. There are also students who take on the voices of cartoon characters or actors or actresses from movies.

When the prosody of a student's voice brings about ridicule or isolation from peers, it is probably a good idea to help this student develop an awareness of how he or she sounds. Tape recorders are good tools to help make the student more aware of the melody of his voice. If you try to record the voice in its normal prosody and also when the student is using unusual voice patterns, this is even more helpful. In this way, you can play back the tape and encourage the student to "hear" the differences. However, even after this direct instruction, there will probably be times "in the moment" when the child will need reminders to help teach these replacement skills. As always, be sure to reinforce the student when he is using appropriate prosody.

Many children with autism also exhibit inappropriate volume or speed in their voice, as mentioned earlier. Drawing a scale on a piece of paper using the numbers 1-3, with "1" being "too slow" and "3" being "too fast," will help teach the student to modulate his or her voice. This same skill can be used to teach "too loud" and "too soft." Drawing a speedometer to include various prosody settings can also be useful. Oftentimes, when a child speaks too loudly or too softly, we correct him by saying, "You are too loud!" or "Speak up!" But neither of these reactions will teach the child replacement skills. Exactly what does "too loud" or "speak up" mean to a student whose understanding of language is often very concrete?

There are also children who will have difficulty hearing how the voice changes to represent different intensities of emotion. For example, consider the various degrees (intensities) of anger. If one were to classify angry voices according to degrees from 1-3, there might be irritation (1), anger (2), and fury (3). If a student has difficulty distinguishing between intensities of the same emotion, he will most likely have problems adjusting his behavior to those different intensities, as well. Thus, a child that thinks his mother is only slightly angry when she is really furious may not adjust his behavior to help remedy the situation. This same child may also have difficulty recognizing how the voice changes subtly during social communication, such as when someone is using sarcasm or when they might be telling a half-truth or "white lie."

Using visual strategies to teach prosody skills is extremely important to the child with autism and will be much more useful than merely trying to explain it to him or her.

Supplies Needed

Tape recorder, with prerecorded phrases in two sets: One set will contain phrases said at different volume levels (1-3). The phrases should be recorded at least 7 seconds apart. Another set will contain prerecorded phrases said at different speed levels (1-3). Again, the phrases should be recorded at least 7 seconds apart.

Two note cards per student, with a short phrase written on each one, as well as a "1," "2," or "3" written underneath.

A laminated numbered scale from 1-3 (one per student), similar to this:

1	2	3

Lesson

1. Say, "Boys and girls, how many of you have ever been told that you speak too loudly or too softly?" (Solicit answers.) "How about too fast or too slow?" (Solicit answers.)

2. "Sometimes, it his helpful to think of 'too loud' or 'too soft' on a scale from 1-3, with '1' being very soft, '2' being just right, and '3' being very loud. The same can be true of speaking too fast and too slowly—'1' would be very slow, '2' would be just right, and '3' would be very fast."

3. "Let's see if we can practice this. I have recorded some phrases on the tape recorder. I am going to give you a three-point scale, and after you listen to the phrase, I want you to point to either the '1,' '2,' or '3' if you think the voice is very soft, just right, or very loud. I will then stop the tape, and we can discuss what you heard. Does anyone have any questions?"

4. Distribute the scales, and then play the recordings. At the end of each recording, stop and ask the children how they ranked the volume of the phrase.

5. Say, "Now, sometimes a voice can be too slow or too fast, as well. I have recorded some additional phrases for you to listen to. When you listen to the voice, decide if the voice is too slow (that would be a '1'), just right (that would be a '2'), or too fast (that would be a '3'). We will discuss each one, just as before."

6. Play the recordings. At the end of each recording, stop and ask the children how they ranked the speed of the phrase.

7. Say, "Now, this time, I want YOU to practice using different volume levels in your OWN voice. I am going to hand you a note card that has a phrase written on it, as well as a '1,' '2,' or '3.' After you read the phrase to yourself and note the volume level, I will ask you if you are ready. When you are ready, I want you to say the phrase at the volume level that is written. For instance, if you have a '1' on your card, you should say the phrase very softly. A '2' would be said at a 'just right' level, and a '3' would be said very loudly. Then, the rest of us will guess whether you used a volume level of '1,' '2,' or

'3.' Does anyone have any questions?"

8. Distribute the note cards. Let each child take a turn, while the others guess the volume levels.

9. Say, "You did a great job! Now, I am going to give you each a new set of note cards. This time, I want you to read the phrase at the *speed level* indicated on the card: '1' means slow, '2' means 'just right,' and '3' means fast. Then, the rest of us will guess whether you used a speed level of '1,' '2,' or '3.' Does anyone have any questions?"

10. Distribute the note cards. Let each child take their turn, while the others guess the speed levels.

11. Say, "Now, if one of your teachers, parents, or friends says to YOU that you are too loud, I want you to remember that it means you are at a '3,' and you should strive to be a '2.' If they say you are talking too softly, that means you are at a '1,' and you need to be at a '2.' The same thing should happen when your teachers, parents, or friends say that you are talking too fast. That means you are at a '3,' and you should strive to be at a '2.' Does anyone have any questions?"

Note: Another prosody activity would be to record some phrases said at different intensity levels and have the students use their three-point scales to rank the intensity of the emotions used. After each set of phrases, you could discuss with the children appropriate response behaviors that would go along with each intensity level. As an example, listening to a voice that sounds sad versus a voice of someone who is sobbing should elicit a different response in the listener.

Lesson 2D
Using "My Turn" Cards to Teach
Refraining from Interrupting

IEP Goal: "When provided with visual prompts, the student will refrain from interrupting in four out of five observations."

General Information

Many children on the autism spectrum have difficulty with understanding the flow of a conversation. They talk "at" you instead of "with" you. They can't grasp the idea that conversations are reciprocal and that people take turns in their exchanges. They also have difficulty understanding that successful conversations have several components:

1. *A topic that both partners enjoy.* Occasionally, one partner may sacrifice his own interest in the topic to make his communication partner feel special. Although the topic is not something he may not enjoy, he stays engaged because *his partner enjoys the topic!*

2. *Interruptions disrupt the flow of the conversation and are often perceived as annoying by communication partners.* The flow is disrupted because many people cannot "disconnect" from their thought processes and "connect" with the interrupter's thought process, and then return to the original conversation easily. This requires a *shifting process* while holding the original conversation in working memory. Many folks with executive-function deficits find this task difficult. Interfering factors at the time of the interruption, such as stress levels and noise, can compound this difficulty.

3. *Interruptions can take the form of questions or comments that are not relevant to the topic.* Many times, kids with autism do not realize that their interruptions are not relevant because they were not paying attention to what was going on at the time they interrupted. Simple, concrete rules, such

as, "Don't interrupt when I am on the phone unless it is important to interrupt" (followed by a list of times when it's OK to interrupt), would be most helpful to the student who has difficulty discerning this.

Just like any other skill, being able to engage in conversations is something that students with autism need to practice. And, just like any other skill, they will get better at it and become more at ease with it as they practice. In the beginning, conversation skills may need to be provided in a one-on-one setting by using topics they enjoy to make them comfortable. Then, students can be given opportunities to practice in controlled group settings as they develop more "tools" for being successful. Gradually, the number of conversational turns can be increased, as well as the topics of discussion. Finally, reinforcing the child's success in everyday social scenarios will be important if the skill will be generalized well to those settings.

Supplies Needed

3 x 5 cards with "My Turn" wording on each (one per student)

Three Popsicle or craft sticks per student

Zip-lock baggie (one per student)

One volume of any encyclopedia set

Lesson

1. Say, "Boys and girls, when you have a conversation with someone, you take turns. It's a lot like playing volleyball. First, when you a start a conversation with someone, you take your turn and throw your conversation ball over the net. Then, the person you are talking to takes a turn and throws the conversation ball back to you." Pass a "My Turn" card back and forth to someone to demonstrate this skill. Or, you could also use a large ball.

2. Say, "People usually do not like it when you interrupt or don't allow them to have a turn when they talk. They may not want to continue talking with you if you don't allow them to have their turn."

3. "We are going to do a little activity now. Let's pretend I am your teacher, and we are in class. I am going to pick a topic. Once I say the topic, you may make a comment or ask a question about that topic, but you have to take turns. So, let's say I choose 'pizza' as the topic. When you have a comment or a question about 'pizza,' raise your 'My Turn' card so I can call on you. *I have to call on you* before you can take your turn." Distribute the "My Turn" cards.

4. Play the game by using various topics. Reinforce kids who are using their "My Turn" cards appropriately, staying on topic, and refraining from interrupting.

5. Say, "The other problem that sometimes happens is when you interrupt a person by asking too many questions. For instance, your teacher may not appreciate when you ask questions just to ask questions. If you *really need* to know the answer, or

you can't do the work because you have a question, then it's OK to ask a question. But if you are asking questions just to interrupt or show how smart you are, then the questions are not necessary and can be annoying to others."

6. Say, "We are going to practice this skill of limiting your questions. I am going to give you three Popsicle sticks and a zip-lock baggie. I will read an article out of an encyclopedia on a topic that you might find interesting. As I read, you should think of three questions to ask me about the topic. When you want to ask a question, raise your hand. When I call on you, you may ask your question and put a Popsicle stick in the zip-lock baggie. When you have put all of your Popsicle sticks into your zip-lock baggie, you may not ask any more questions."

7. Choose various topics from the encyclopedia to read to the students. Reinforce the students who raise their hands and take their turns.

Note: There are various ways that students with autism interrupt in the classroom. Some do so by calling out. Others do so by complaining. Empty Kleenex boxes could be used as "complaint" boxes. Kids could be encouraged to write their complaints on slips of paper and insert those slips into the complaint box for review later. You can also use the same concept for excessive numbers of questions. Once the allotted number of questions has been asked, the student can be encouraged to write additional questions on slips of paper and place them in the Kleenex box. The questions can be reviewed at another, more convenient time. Remember, too, that some children ask questions to get the teacher's attention. When these questions are honored, these students gain attention, thus reinforcing the behavior. It is more likely that this will result in even more questions. Therefore, limiting the number of interruptions by providing the student with controlled opportunities to interrupt can certainly be helpful in regulating this type of behavior.

Lesson 2E
Using a Traffic Light to Teach Students to Monitor Their Perseverative Talk

IEP Goal: "When given a visual prompt (a traffic light), the student will demonstrate the ability to avoid perseverative talk in four out of five opportunities."

General Information

Many children with autism engage in perseverative talk, which is talk that is centered around one particular subject area. Usually, what makes the perseverative talk unusual is *(a)* how much the student engages in such behavior and *(b)* that the topic is either not age appropriate or a topic that peers would find interesting.

Perseverations are a symptom of brain dysfunction, and children with autism are not the only ones that engage in this type of behavior. Individuals with dementia or Alzheimer disease frequently have perseverations. Children with obsessive-compulsive disorder and Tourette syndrome can also perseverate.

Since perseverations can interfere with many aspects of daily life, it is important to have the student become aware of his perseverations and how much he or she is engaging in this behavior. An appropriate goal for the student would be to learn that there is a time and a place for perseverations and that he or she can often self-monitor this behavior.

Traffic lights are everywhere. They provide us with a concrete way to manage our driving behavior. Just about everyone is familiar with the framework of rules they provide for us: "Green" means go, "red" commands us to stop, and "yellow" means caution.

If we use the traffic light as our visual, one would think that the color that would work best for controlling perseverations would be "red." But, in applied behavior analysis, "green" would actually have the most power to change behavior *(any behavior that is reinforced is most likely to increase).*

"Yellow" lights have a power of their own—they encourage the student to engage in self-reflection. In the end, both "yellow" and "green" will bring about positive change in the student who perseverates.

Zip-lock baggies can also be useful in helping a student learn that there is a time and a place for perseverations. With the use of a visual schedule, you can give the student daily opportunities to engage in such activities; then, zipping the visual of the perseveration in a zip-lock baggie will "show" him that it's not time for train talk or train play (or whatever the topic of perseveraion is), but there will be time for such behavior later in the day. Showing the "perseveration time" on a visual schedule is helpful—this encourages the student to "wait" for his predetermined time.

We all have special interests and hobbies that we like to do in our spare time. When we're working, however, we can't engage in Facebook, plan out how our garden will look, or shop for clothes online. Work is work, and play is play. Our children need to learn the difference, as well, so they can act appropriately with peers and in their classrooms at school.

Supplies Needed

3 x 5 laminated stoplight cards (Using red, yellow, and green circle stickers, create some note cards that are "red lights," some that are green, and some that are yellow.)

Lots of Legos or other building-type toys (You will be dividing the group into pairs, and each pair will need enough Legos to complete a project.)

You may also need to ask for the assistance of another adult to help you monitor the flow of various conversations that the kids will have with each other.

Lesson

1. Say, "Boys and girls, today we are going to talk about an important skill that will help to make our conversations with others more meaningful. First, I am going to ask you, what is your favorite thing to do in your spare time?" (Solicit answers from the kids.)

2. "Well those are all pretty cool things! But, I am sure you know that everyone has favorite things that they like to do. I enjoy _____ (fill in the blank). But, I also have a job to do here, as well. If I allowed myself to do _____ while I was at work, I could lose my job! Why do you think that is?" (Solicit answers from the kids.)

3. "So, you have to understand that there is a time and a place for your special activities."

4. "When you are speaking with someone, there is one rule that you should try to remember, and it is this: *People like to talk about things THEY like or enjoy.* What does that mean?" (Solicit answers from the kids.)

5. "When you are having a conversation with someone, you should try to remember that the person you are talking to has special interests, too. You should try to give them a turn to talk about their interests. Being a friend means that you should try to value what it is your friend likes, as well."

6. "Today, during our class, we are going to work together to make some Lego buildings. I will put you in groups of two to do that. While you are working, I want you to talk with each other about the things that you enjoy, but at the same time, I want you to listen to what the other person enjoys, too. If you are doing a good job of engaging in topics that your partners like, I am going to give you a green light. If you start to talk too much about topics YOU like, I might give you a yellow light. The yellow light means that you should think about what you are saying and try to let your partner talk a little bit, too. Yellow lights means 'Caution!' You may be running into trouble! Red lights mean you need to STOP! Does everyone understand?"

7. Put the kids in groups of two and provide each group with building materials.

8. As the kids engage in play, the adults should listen to the various conversations. When a kid is doing a good job of avoiding perseverative talk, give him a green-light card. If he or another child begins to engage in perseverative talk, provide this child with a yellow-light card and remind him or her to monitor his or her talk. If, after two reminders, he or she is unable to do this, pull the child away from the group to discuss what went wrong. Show him or her that this is "red-light" time. Remember, it is more important to provide green lights than red lights. We want the children to feel successful at having conversations. You may want to avoid actually distributing red lights, as this may make anxious children even more stressed about engaging in conversations.

Unit 3
Working Successfully with Others

Lesson 3A
Using Name Tags to Become
Aware of Group Roles

IEP Goal: "When each group member is given a job-title tag to wear, as well as a task list to complete a job, the student will be able to complete his task list in four out of five group activities."

General Information

It is the common complaint of many teachers that students do not know how to work successfully in groups. Many children on the spectrum will resort to engaging in self-stimulatory behavior or other inappropriate behavior when asked to complete a project with peers. It is almost as if they don't understand the group's dynamics.

Children with autism are not the only ones who struggle at times when given group assignments. There is often a child who will "overfunction" in a group setting—meaning he or she will take over the project and complete not only his or her portion, but others', as well. There is also the child who doesn't seem to contribute to the workload enough. This student may be perceived by the other group members as being lazy or not "doing his fair share."

All of these children need direct instruction on the roles that people play in groups. They are not properly gleaning their particular role in the group dynamic with regard to completing the assigned project. These children require adult intervention if they are to become contributing members of their teams.

Possible roles that students can fulfill in a group setting are the following:

Power Point developer	Typist
Presenter	Special effects
Editor	Suggestion maker
Supply coordinator	Timekeeper
Props	Note taker
Costumes	Photocopier
Artist	Musician

When the roles are designated clearly and students are provided with a task list to complete their own roles, many are able to become contributing members of the group. Indeed, their contributions often become valuable.

"Name tags" can be made out of laminated note cards with holes punched into two corners and a string or ribbon affixed through the holes. This allows them to be worn around the neck. It is important that the other students in the group wear their tags as well, so the student with autism can understand his role in relationship to others. Making the task lists of the other students available to him or her can also be helpful.

Supplies Needed

3 x 5 note cards (three for each student)

Yarn or ribbon (about 2½ feet per child)

A couple of one-hole punchers for group members to share

A magic marker and a pencil for each student

Legos or other building materials (Lincoln Logs, Tinker Toys, Erector Sets), enough for each group of three kids to have a sizeable amount

Lesson

1.   Provide each student with two note cards, about 2½ feet of ribbon, and a magic marker.

2.   Say, "Boys and girls, when you work in a group to complete a project or assignment, you should each have a role, as well as a list of things to do to be a contributing member of the group. Some people like to do too much, and some people don't do enough. Each of you has strengths or special skills you do well. Those things could be great for you to do for the group, too! For instance, some of you are really good at art. Your role in a group project, then, could be to design all the work. Some of you are really good on the computer. Your role, then, could be to design the Power Point presentation or create the graphics."

3.   Say, "I am going to make a list of all the possible roles or jobs that people do in a group on the board. You should read the list and see if you can think of any others." Write the list from the previous page on the board. If you can think of additional ones to add, write those on the board, as well. Solicit student contributions. Go over what each role is so all students understand the function of these roles.

4.   Say, "On one of the cards I have given you, I would like you to write ONE of the roles on the board that you think you could do if you were in a group. Then, on a second card, I want you to write ANOTHER role that you think you could do." Assist the students in making two of their most desirable choices from those offered, and write one on each card.

5. Say, "Now I am going to help you select a role from the two that you think you could do." Help the students to select a role, and try to avoid duplication.

6. Say, "We are now going to make a name tag to wear each time we work in a group setting so everyone in the group knows each other's roles."

7. Have the students select one of the cards that designates a role he wishes to fulfill in the group. Use the hole-puncher to punch a hole in the top corner of each side of the card. Thread a piece of ribbon or yarn into one of the holes and secure it with a knot so it doesn't slide through the hole. String the other end of the yarn or ribbon through the other hole, tying a knot in the same fashion. The student should now be able to hang the name tag around his neck so all can see the role he has selected.

8. Say, "Now, we are going to begin a group project shortly, but first we are going to review what everyone has selected as their role for the project." Go around the room and review the chosen roles.

9. Say, "With the last note card, I would like you to take a pencil and write at least three or four jobs that you think you should do to complete your role. For instance, if I decided to be the props coordinator, I might have the following jobs:

    A. Write down the props that the team has decided to use on a piece of paper.

    B. Gather the props from home, a local store, or a thrift shop.

C.   Check off the props that have been located and bring them to school.

D.   Make a list of other props that could not be located and bring this list to school.

E.   Ask other group members if they may be able to locate these props.

You may want to develop another list on the board for an additional role the students have not chosen.

10.   Assist each student in writing three tasks on the note card that he or she could do to complete his or her role. Have the student write his name on the back of his name tag and his note card and collect them after each group meeting. Redistribute them at the start of each group meeting. You should require that the students wear the name tags so everyone in the group becomes familiar with the various roles that other students play in the completion of the project. For older kids, you can make note cards that are similar to placeholders— the cards are folded in half and made to "stand up" on the desk or table in front of where the student is sitting. If you select this type of name tag, the cards should be about as big as a full-sized piece of paper so they can be folded.

11.   With the Legos or other building materials, create a project for the students to collaborate on. For instance, maybe the kids can use their Legos to create a building. After the building is completed, they will need someone to draw a picture or blueprint of it and have someone present what

the building is and how it would be used. Another person could write the supplies that are required to complete it, and so on.

For the next group session, develop and assign group projects that would be compatible with the roles that the students selected to maximize the participation of the group members.

Lesson 3B
Using Colored Cellophane to Become Aware of Others' Viewpoints

IEP Goal: "When given instruction with colored cellophane, the student will be able to successfully state the viewpoints or perspectives of at least one other person in four out of five social scenarios."

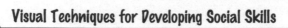

General Information

Students with autism often lack the ability to recognize the perspectives of others. They can't seem to understand that others have different viewpoints. This may give rise to several social "sticky points." For instance, many kids struggle with the following perspective-related issues:

- Understanding when something is an accident versus when it's done on purpose

- Distinguishing between friendly teasing versus harmful teasing

- Laughing with you rather than at you

- Recognizing a friendship versus a romantic interest

- Exhibiting stalking-type behaviors

- Identifying a friend versus an acquaintance

Teenagers, in particular, often lack the social awareness to understand when someone is being nice to them for the sake of friendship, versus being nice to them because they are interested romantically. When they misinterpret these types of social signals, their behavior may begin to cross over into "stalking."

If one asks the victim of stalking what it is that disturbs him/her about the behavior of his/her stalker, there are generally two threads:

1. It's not reciprocated.

2. The frequency of contact is inappropriate.

A student who is engaging in stalking-type behavior will have to learn that frequency is a concern, and the number of his interactions with the person(s) being "stalked" will have to be curbed. We can sometimes achieve this by giving the student a zip-lock baggie and providing him with a minimum number of "opportunity cards" to record the date and time of interaction and having him put a used opportunity card in the baggie to seal up. If he is able to keep the opportunity cards at the appropriate number, he can earn a reinforcer, but if he has leftover cards, he earns an even more valuable reinforcer. *Remember—any behavior that's reinforced is likely to continue!*

Teenagers aren't the only ones who seem to lack the ability to take others' perspectives into account. An observer can easily see problems ascertaining perspectives in any given school day by listening to children at play. Oftentimes, this type of behavior can be observed at recess or during class as the children participate in games. Some children will be inappropriate with their behavior not only when they lose, but also when they win!

Another type of problem with perspectives is having an understanding of the difference between friends and acquaintances. Friendships can be confusing to children on the spectrum. When asked to list their best friends, they will often list children that are in their class or those who live in their neighborhood—or possibly even relatives. But, their parents will say that they don't go to these children's homes to play, get invited to their parties, or talk with them on the telephone or through electronic communications. Clearly, they are misinterpreting the level of intimacy they have with these children, and thus the type of relationship they have. The kids that they think are friends are really nothing more than acquaintances.

Considering others' perspectives is one of the most difficult skills to teach. It requires the ability to read facial expressions and gestures, possess a certain degree of empathy, as well as have a desire to connect with someone else's feelings. Having the motivation to put forth the effort may also play a part in how well some children will be able to master this skill. For some kids with autism who have had difficult experiences with prior social relationships, motivation may be a hindrance in their ability to develop intimate relationships with others.

For this student, it will be helpful to keep social interactions short in duration, design an activity that would be highly interesting to the student (an activity centered around his/her special interest), and reinforce the student's participation afterward, to slowly increase the desired number of minutes he or she can participate in future activities before earning the reinforcer. If the student is still reluctant, before the activity occurs, discuss with him what desirable reinforcer he would like to earn upon completion of the social task. Keep the social task list short and pleasurable.

TOURO COLLEGE LIBRARY

Supplies Needed

Small, 2-inch squares of cellophane in different colors (If cellophane is hard to find, using sunglasses with differently colored lenses may serve the same purpose.)

Wipe-off board and markers, or a chalkboard and chalk

Note cards with short scenarios (One per group member—the scenarios depict a character who struggles with a social problem. Perhaps a student has missed his bus or forgotten his lunch or is getting a sore throat. The students are going to guess how the person feels in the story by attempting to discover the character's perspective.)

Pictures from magazines that show a social perspective (One per group member—for instance, a woman attending a funeral, a man sitting in church, or an employee looking exhausted.)

One or two other adults to assist with the role-playing activity of this lesson plan (depending on how many students are in the group)

Optional: Video camera and/or TV set

Lesson

1. Say, "Boys and girls, how many of you have ever looked through a piece of colored cellophane or sunglasses that have differently colored lenses?" (Solicit responses.) "It's pretty cool, isn't it? Let's try it now."

2. Distribute pieces of colored cellophane or sunglasses to the group members. Try to hand out at least three different colors of each.

3. Say, "Now, I want you to hold up your cellophane (or sunglasses) to your eyes, and tell me what you see when you look at this." Choose an object as a frame of reference for everyone to look at, such as a flowerpot, a picture, or a chair. What you are attempting to do is establish a frame of reference, in which every child is looking at the object but in a different way.

4. Say, "Now, I want you to take turns telling me exactly what you see when I point to this object."

5. Solicit answers, but encourage the kids to describe the object and the color of the object. If you want, have kids trade colors of cellophane and try the activity again.

6. Say, "That's right! You all see the same chair (or flowerpot or picture), but in a different color. The colors are like viewpoints. Some of you are seeing things in a red way, a green way, a yellow way, or a blue way. Everyone has different perceptions of things. There is no way to understand everyone's perspective exactly, because you can't crawl into

their heads and see out of their eyes. But, there are certainly ways that you can try to understand perspectives. Let's write these on the board."

7. List the following boldface items on the board to discuss with the students:

- **You have had a similar experience yourself.** Share with the students an experience that you have had and ask them if they have ever had the experience, too. Emphasize that it is something they have in common with you. So, whenever you talk about the experience, you are likely to have a similar viewpoint (ie, color) with someone who has also had that experience.

- **You have heard about someone who had a similar experience.** Sometimes you can carry knowledge you have about an experience over to the current situation and be able to understand what it feels like. Give some examples. For instance, maybe you saw your sister get stung by a bee, but you have never been stung. You remember that she was in a great deal of pain, so you can relate to someone else who gets stung by a bee. Or, perhaps you never have been to a circus, but you saw a movie about it one time and know what it's like.

- **You can imagine what it feels like to feel the way the person is feeling, because you can "put yourself" into their experience.** This might be a good opportunity to discuss the idiom "stepping into someone's shoes" and what it means. Give some examples. For instance, someone is crying because their pet has died. Although this has never happened to you, if you think about never being able to see your own pet again, it would make you sad.

8. Say, "Now, we are going to practice understanding viewpoints. I am going to give each of you a card that has a little story about something that is happening to someone else. I want you to use the three things I've written on the board to figure out how the person may be feeling in the story. I will help you." Go around to each group, helping them to understand the character's perspective in the story on their cards.

9. Say, "Let's take turns reading the stories out loud and describing how the character in the story feels." Each student should take a turn reading his card. Encourage discussion among the group members— especially if there are different perspectives. Emphasize that these are like the various "colors" of cellophane and that there are no wrong answers, because we can't crawl into the mind of the person in the story and know how he feels for sure. We are only making guesses...but some guesses are better than others.

10. Distribute the pictures. Have the students take turns identifying how the people in the pictures are feeling. You may have to emphasize facial expressions and other aspects of the picture that could provide clues.

11. Say, "Now, up to this point, we have worked on understanding the perspectives of only one person in a picture or in a story. Now, let's try understanding several people's perspectives. Let's role-play some situations that happen very frequently in school."

12. Assign the children to various areas to work on a small skit in which these types of social scenarios are depicted. The children will act them out in front of the group, and you should serve as a facilitator to help them see the various viewpoints (ie, "colors") of each actor in the group. Writing the viewpoints on the board may be helpful! If the students have created a good skit, consider videotaping the skit for use later. Research tells us that children always learn best from videotapes that depict their peers and/or themselves.

Here are some potential scenarios to use for the skits:

- Some kids are playing a board game, and one child wins. The child brags, dances around, and displays poor sportsmanship.

- After playing a board game, one child is a sore loser.

- A student reacts inappropriately to friendly teasing.

- A child butts in line and refuses to take his turn.

- A student has received a bad score on his test. Another student keeps asking him what he got, not noticing that the first student doesn't want to tell him his score.

- A student is waiting his turn to use the glue, while the student who has the glue takes his time, laughs, and chats with friends, ignoring the other student's needs.

- One student gets pushed into another deliberately. Then you can use scenario again, but this time, depict it as an accident.

- Two students are playing a video game, where one is shouting out verbal threats to the other: "I'm going to kill you! You are going to get shot to pieces!" Then you can use this scenario again, but this time, there is no video game. One student merely approaches another and says the same words in an angry tone, in an inappropriate setting.

Lesson 3C
Using a Chain to Teach
Understanding Consequences

IEP Goal: "When given a chain and a problematic social situation, the student will be able to describe the sequence of events that led to the outcome in four out of five observations."

General Information

Children with autism often lack the ability to sequence the steps required for task completion. In reading-comprehension activities, educators often observe that listing the order of events in a story is a difficult task for a student with autism. This "task-sequencing" ability often requires direct instruction by using a step-by-step visual organizer for the student to be able to see how sequences affect outcomes.

This same problem becomes evident in the social world, too. Many children are unable to see the steps that lead to a social problem. Understanding how many social problems result from a failure to grasp the sequence of events can be difficult for students with autism to process. This, coupled with a deficit in the ability to see others' perspectives, can really add up to some confusing social scenarios!

If your student (or child) with autism has difficulty with sequencing, consider using a chain-link visual to analyze the steps of everyday processes from start to completion. Take, for example, the task of washing clothes. For clothes to become clean, there are several items that have to be accomplished in a set fashion to complete the "chain links" of washing clothes:

- Sort the clothes by color.

- Put them in the washing machine.

- Add detergent.

- Choose the appropriate temperature setting, load capacity, and spin cycle.

109

- Remove the clothes from the washer to dry them, either in a dryer or on a clothesline.

- If in a dryer, perhaps add a dryer sheet.

- Choose the appropriate settings for temperature, load capacity, and time.

- If on a clothesline, hang the items on the line with clothespins.

- When the clothes are dry, fold them neatly.

- Put them away or hang them up in the appropriate place.

Using visuals in the form of pictures or task lists to teach students with autism can help them learn to complete tasks in a step-by-step fashion. Similarly, this "chain-link" technique can be useful for teaching them what they must do to be socially appropriate, too! For instance, consider these steps involved in making a playdate:

- Choose a peer to play with.

- Pick a date and time that is acceptable to your parents. Ask how the peer will get to your home, how he will go home, and what time this will occur (if necessary, write it down).

- Call the peer and say, "Hey, can you come over on (date and time) for a while?" Give your peer the information from your parents on how or she will arrive and depart.

- Get ready for the peer: Plan snacks, drinks, and three activities you could do together.

- When the peer arrives, greet him by saying, "Hey, thanks for coming!"

- Ask the peer which of the three activities he would like to do. If he doesn't want to do any of them, ask him what he would like to do instead.

- Play for a half-hour, and then ask if he wants a drink or a snack.

- Eat the snack or continue playing.

As students get older, they must begin to understand that what they do affects others and sets a chain of events in motion. Sometimes the chain can lead to a successful social outcome. Other times, the chain is broken if the student fails to complete a necessary action to keep the chain together or engages in an activity that causes the chain to break. If we can show children visually how to keep a social chain from breaking, they will be more likely to experience success in their social relationships. Every unsuccessful social experience can become a learning tool for a future one. Analyzing unsuccessful social interactions by using a chain-link approach can also be helpful! Rather than punishing the child for being inappropriate, the chain-link analogy can visually show the outcome as it would occur in a more successful way, had the student been more appropriate in his actions.

Supplies Needed

A plastic chain-link toy (This is available at Wal-Mart and can be called "Mister Chain" or "EduShape Chain Links." It is helpful to get at least two or three packages with different colors.)

Note cards with everyday tasks that involve a sequence (Write one task on each card, such as starting a dishwasher, making a bed, brushing your teeth, or making cereal.)

Note cards with problematic social scenarios at school (Write one problem per card, such as making a rude comment, not doing homework, not helping in a group, or bragging after winning a game.)

Chalkboard and chalk or a wipe-off board with markers and erasers

Several handouts for each student with a large chain drawn down the middle that provides many links large enough to write in (Make an overhead transparency of this same handout.)

An overhead projector and marker

Lesson

Note: This lesson plan may take one or more sessions to complete.

1.   Say, "Sometimes, people think that their actions as they go through the day do not affect the actions of others. They think that things happen accidentally, but it's really the opposite. Things happen for a reason. What you say and do can have an effect on what happens next."

2.   "Let's think about some everyday tasks that we do." Pass out a note card with one everyday task written on it, such as making a bed or brushing your teeth.

3.   Hold up the chain links individually and ask someone to read what is written on their card. Say, "Your task cannot get done unless things occur in a certain order, isn't that right?"

4.   On the board, write the sequence of steps required to complete the task written on someone's card. Use your chain links to demonstrate that you are adding links, one by one, as the sequence is detailed on the board. You could actually draw large links and write the steps in the middle of each link.

5.   Do the same with what is written on someone else's card.

6.   Ask the students who have already completed their assignment to work in pairs with the remaining students in the group.

7.   Say, "Now, social and school processes work the same way. Let's start all over and talk about the

steps you follow in the morning to get ready to come to school." Build a single-color chain to depict each step while writing the steps on the board.

8. Say, "What do you think would happen if one of these steps were missed, or if one of the steps had happened in a different way?" On the chalkboard, go back to the step that is going to change and make an arrow to a clean place on the blackboard to start a new series of steps from the identified link.

9. Demonstrate how to use the chain by showing the link that is going to have TWO links in it...one will continue the chain as previously discussed, but the other will be used to develop a new chain of events. Use a second color for the new series of steps.

10. Say, "What do you think will be the order of steps now that we have changed this one link?" Develop on the board a new series of adjusted "steps." Use the new color of links to demonstrate how the new links are being added accordingly.

11. Say, "Do you see how one change can make a difference and how you can make a whole new outcome of events by making that one little change?"

12. "Now, let's talk about a problem you may be having at home. Who remembers the last time your mom or dad got mad at you? What were they mad about?" Solicit responses. If there are none, talk about a common problem that occurs at home, such as cleaning their room. Discuss the chain that develops if they clean their room versus if their mom or dad has to clean their room for them. Discuss how feelings affect this and how consequences arise that may not be pleasant for the student. (Perhaps

things get thrown away that they still want, or Mom gets grumpy, or the student gets punished for not doing what he was asked to do.) What you are striving for is to help the students see the outcomes of their actions.

13. Distribute cards that list school-related problems and a chain-link handout for each student.

14. Have the students write on the handout while you complete it with them on the overhead projector. You should depict the series of steps on the social scenario card they were given. Put a star beside the "critical" link to the left of the link and draw a new series of chain-link steps to the right to show how the scenario could end better.

15. Give the students new handouts and have them work together on the other scenario cards. Go over these on the overhead projector when they are done.

Note: When problematic social situations occur for the student in the future, the chain-link lesson is an excellent way to work with the student to retrace the steps of how the situation occurred. Then, you can help the student refashion them so he can learn what might have been a more appropriate choice.

In Closing

Temple Grandin is perhaps the most well-known person with autism alive today. In her enlightening book, *Thinking in Pictures: My Life with Autism,* she stated the following:

> Unlike those of most people, my thoughts move from video, like specific images to generalization and concepts. For example, my concept of dogs is inextricably linked to every dog I've ever known. It's as if I have a card catalog of dogs I have seen, complete with pictures, which continually grows as I add more examples to my video library. If I think about Great Danes, the first memory that pops into my head is Dansk, the Great Dane owned by the headmaster at my high school. The next Great Dane I visualize is Helga, who was Dansk's replacement. The next is my aunt's dog in Arizona, and my final image comes from an advertisement for Fitwell seat covers that featured that kind of dog. My memories usually appear in my imagination in strict chronological order, and the images I visualize are always specific. There is no generic, generalized Great Dane.

After reading several of Temple Grandin's books and watching my own son struggle with the daily tasks the rest of us find so mundane, I began to "see the light."

As educators and parents, we simply must continue (and in some cases begin!) the process of working with children who have autism spectrum disorders in the manner that best addresses their individual learning styles. We must take our own preconceived notions out of the mix. Only when we connect with them at the core center of their uniqueness can we even hope to make a difference in their young lives.

Rebecca Moyes

About the Author

Rebecca Moyes, MEd, was a regular-education teacher in public and private schools in Pennsylvania for 9 years. After her son was diagnosed with a disability, she left her teaching position to become an inclusion consultant. Today, she serves as the director of the Pressley Ridge School for Autism in Pittsburgh, Pennsylvania. She also provides consultation and training to school districts. She speaks at seminars with the Bureau of Education Research in cities throughout the United States and is highly recognized as an authority in the field of autism education. She is also an educational advocate for students with disabilities.

Rebecca is the author of four books: *Incorporating Social Goals in the Classroom—A Guide for Teachers and Parents of Children with High Functioning Autism and Asperger's Syndrome* was published in 2001. Her second book, *Addressing the Challenging Behavior of Children with High Functioning Autism and Asperger's Syndrome in the Classroom,* came out in 2002. Her third book, which was published by Future Horizons, received the I-Parenting Award. It is titled, *I Need Help with School.* This book helps parents write effective IEPs for their children. Her fourth book, *Building Sensory Friendly Classrooms to Support Children with Challenging Behaviors: Implementing Data Driven Strategies!,* was published by Sensory World in 2010.

Rebecca has two children, who are both currently in college. In her spare time, she enjoys reading and gardening.

Rebecca can be contacted through Future Horizons or by e-mail at *bmoyes123@aol.com.*

Additional Resources

1001 Great Ideas for Teaching and Raising Children with Autism or Asperger's, Revised and Expanded 2nd Edition
by Ellen Notbohm and Veronica Zysk
ISBN: 9781935274063

Answers to Questions Teachers Ask about Sensory Integration: Forms, Checklists, and Practical Tools
by Carol Kranowitz and Stacey Szklut
ISBN: 9781932565461

Basic Skills Checklists: Teacher-friendly Assessment for Students with Autism or Special Needs
by Marlene Breitenbach
ISBN: 9781932565751

The CAT-kit: The new Cognitive Affective Training program for improving communication!
by Tony Attwood, Kirsten Callesen, and Annette Moller Nielson
ISBN: 9781932565737

Building Bridges through Sensory Integration: Therapy for Children with Autism and Other Pervasive Developmental Disorders
by Paula Aquilla and Shirley Sutton
ISBN: 9781932565454

How Do I Teach This Kid? Visual Work Tasks for Beginning Learners on the Autism Spectrum
by Kimberly Henry
ISBN: 9781932565249

Inclusive Programming for Elementary Students with Autism
by Sheila Wagner
ISBN: 9781885477545

Inclusive Programming for High School Students with Autism or Asperger's Syndrome
by Sheila Wagner
ISBN: 9781932565577

Inclusive Programming for Middle School Students with Autism or Asperger's Syndrome
by Sheila Wagner
ISBN: 9781885477842

Learning in Motion: 101+ Sensory Activities for the Classroom
by Patricia Angermeier and Joan Krzyzanowski
ISBN: 9781932565904

My Friend with Autism: A Children's Book for Peers
by Beverly Bishop and Craig Bishop
ISBN: 9781885477897

The New Social Story Book, Revised and Expanded 10th Anniversary Edition: Over 150 Social Stories that Teach Everyday Social Skills to Children with Autism or Asperger's Syndrome, and Their Peers
by Carol Gray
ISBN: 9781935274056

No More Meltdowns: Positive Strategies for Managing and Preventing Out-of-Control Behavior
by Jed Baker
ISBN: 9781932565621

Sensitive Sam: Sam's Sensory Adventure Has a Happy Ending!
by Marla Roth-Fisch
ISBN: 9781932565867

Social Skills Training for Children and Adolescents with Asperger Syndrome and Social-Communications Problems
by Jed Baker
ISBN: 9781931282208

Squirmy Wormy: How I Learned to Help Myself
by Lynda Farrington Wilson
ISBN: 9781935567189

The Social Skills Picture Book: Teaching Play, Emotion, and Communication to Children with Autism
by Jed Baker
ISBN: 9781885477910

Ten Things Every Child with Autism Wishes You Know
by Ellen Notbohm
ISBN: 9781932565300

Ten Things Your Student with Autism Wishes You Knew
by Ellen Notbohm
ISBN: 9781932565362

A Treasure Chest of Behavioral Strategies for Individuals with Autism
by Beth Fouse and Maria Wheeler
ISBN: 9781885477361

Ultimate Guide to Sensory Processing Disorder: Easy, Everyday Solutions to Sensory Challenges
by Roya Ostovar
ISBN: 9781935274070

Understanding Asperger's Syndrome, Fast Facts: A Guide for Teachers and Educators to Address the Needs of the Student
by Emily Burrows and Sheila Wagner
ISBN: 9781932565157

All resources are available in fine bookstores everywhere and on the publisher's Web site www.FHautism.com.

Index

H

L

I